Dad You're Pandastic

Written and Illustrated by
Jonathan Hill

Get Free Color by Number book send a Mail
After Purchase to info@harbourhousepress.co.uk

Dedicated to My Wife:
Catherine

Harbour
HOUSE PUBLISHING LTD

Dad, you're the
MANE man in my
life!

Dad, you're a **BEAR**y strong pillar in my life!

You're the G.O.A.T.,
Dad - Greatest Of All
Time!

To the most
HOPtacular dad, you
always make me
smile!

Dad, I WHALE
Always Love you, you
are my Role Model.

To the most
BULLmazing dad
who makes every day
special!

You're one in a CROCODILLION, Dad!

You've always been a DUCKtastic dad, and I love you!

Thanks for always being a DOLPHINitely great father!

Dad, you're an **EAGLE**ent father, soaring above the rest!

Dad, your love is as vast as the GIRAFFE's reach, and I cherish it!

You're such an OWLstanding dad, and I'm so lucky to have you!

Dad, you're totally **PAW**some and I'm not LION!

Dad, you're truly a
PHEASANT surprise
in my life!

You're the SEALy
best, Dad, and I'm
forever grateful!

Dad, you're a true TIGERiffic role model!

Thanks
DAD

Made in United States
Orlando, FL
14 June 2023

34143560R00022